POETRY BASICS

○

HAIKU

○

VALERIE BODDEN

SAUNDERS
BOOK COMPANY

Paperback edition published in 2010 by Saunders Book Company
27 Stewart Road, Collingwood, ON Canada L9Y 4M7

Design and production by Stephanie Blumenthal
Printed in the United States of America

Photographs by Alamy (Phillip Augustavo, Mary Evans Picture Library), The Bridgeman Art Library
(Elizabeth Mowry, Ran-Koo, Nora Summers), Corbis (Artkey, Bettmann, Blue Lantern Studio, Christie's
Images, Sakamoto Photo Research Laboratory), Dreamstime (Kornwa), Getty Images (Aleksandr
Alekseevich Borisov, DEA Picture Library, Nat Farbman//Time & Life Pictures, William Hogarth,
Katsushika Hokusai, Koson Ohara, Li Shan), The Granger Collection, New York; Library of Congress

Library and Archives Canada Cataloguing in Publication
Bodden, Valerie.
Haiku / by Valerie Bodden.
p. cm. — (Poetry basics)
Includes bibliographical references and index.
ISBN 978-1-926722-44-3
1. Haiku—Juvenile literature. 2. Haiku—Authorship—Juvenile literature.
I. Title. II. Series: Bodden, Valerie. Poetry Basics.

PL729.B63 2009
j808.1'41   C2009-902967-7

CG 03/04/10 PO002108
2 4 6 8 9 7 5 3

People have written poems for thousands of years. Long ago, when people wanted to tell a story, they made it into a poem. Today, people write poems about all kinds of topics, from sunsets to traffic jams. Poems can help readers see things in a new way. They can make readers laugh or cry, sigh or scream. The goal of the Japanese form of poetry called haiku is to help readers feel the emotion of a poem by presenting them with a brief image.

Haiku developed out of an even older form of Japanese poetry called *renga*, or "linked verse." This type of poetry began in the 1100s, and by the 1600s, it had become popular among Japan's **middle class**. Groups of about seven or eight people gathered together for renga parties, where they took turns writing the short **stanzas** of a renga.

Before they arrived at the party, each person would write a *hokku*, or opening verse, for the renga. The hokku had to consist of three units of five, seven, and five *onji*, or sound symbols (somewhat similar to English **syllables**). The hokku also had to describe the season during which the poem took place.

One of the great renga masters was a 17th-century poet named Matsuo Basho, who traveled from town to town, teaching people how to write renga. Basho developed the hokku into a beautiful art form and sometimes wrote hokku that weren't expanded into renga. The following hokku by Basho remains the best-known Japanese poem today.

Old Pond — frogs jumped in — sound of water

After Basho, other great Japanese masters of hokku emerged, including 18th-century poets Yosa Buson and Kobayashi Issa. Then, at the end of the 19th century, poet Masaoka Shiki gave the new name "haiku" to hokku that were written to stand on their own. Shiki is considered the first modern haiku poet.

At the beginning of the 1900s, the haiku form was introduced to the **West**. A number of Japanese haiku were translated into French and English. By the time World War I ended in 1918, haiku had begun to draw the attention of poets in Europe and America.

In the United States, poets known as Imagists were strongly influenced by haiku. Imagists used clear, simple **imagery** to show their readers a single moment, just as haiku did. The 1919 poem "Autumn Haze" by Imagist Amy Lowell presents an image of water in the mist. It is among the earliest haiku published in America.

Is it a dragonfly or a maple leaf
That settles softly down upon the water?

Other poets of Lowell's day, including Ezra Pound, William Carlos Williams, and Wallace Stevens, also wrote haiku. By the 1950s, haiku had grown in popularity in the U.S. Today, haiku is one of the most popular forms of poetry in the world. It is written by people in Asia, the Americas, Europe, Australia, and Africa. As each group adds its own unique touches, the form continues to develop.

Ezra Pound

Amy Lowell

Haiku is the shortest poetic form in the world. In Japanese, most haiku are 3 to 10 words long. Like earlier hokku, Japanese haiku traditionally consist of a total of 17 onji divided into groups of 5, 7, and 5.

In English, the rules for haiku are not as strict as in Japanese. Many of the first English-language haiku poets wrote their haiku in 17 syllables divided into lines of 5, 7, and 5 syllables. Today, some poets still choose to follow this form. Count the number of syllables in each line of the haiku on the opposite page. (To count syllables, it sometimes helps to clap each time you say a new complete sound; for example, "po-ta-to" has three syllables.)

Gusting autumn wind
blows shadows from the dark night
leaf-smell underfoot

芭蕉の句碑

「あかあかと日は難面も秋の風」

一六八九（元禄二）年芭蕉が
金沢で作った句である
書は江戸後期金沢の俳人
梅室の筆による

A Haiku by Bashō
Written in Kanazawa in 1689.

Today, many poets of haiku in English no longer try to write three lines of five, seven, and five syllables. This is because English syllables are not exactly the same as Japanese onji. All onji take about the same amount of time to say. But English syllables have very different lengths. As a result, most English-language haiku are shorter than 17 syllables and do not have a set number of syllables per line. Although most haiku are still written in three lines, some poets write one-, two-, or even four-line haiku.

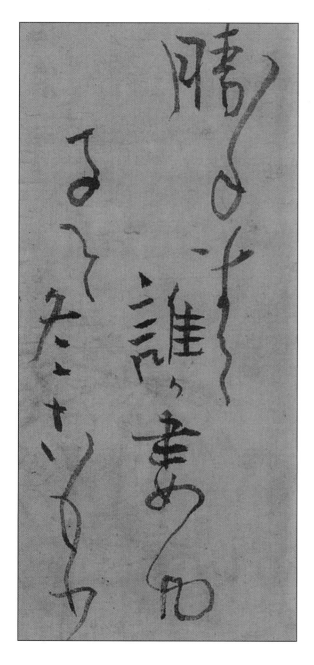

No matter how many lines long they are, most haiku have a break, or pause, at the end of either the first or second line. This break adds emphasis and separates two thoughts or images in the haiku. In Japanese, the pause is indicated with a *kireji*, or cutting word. A cutting word is a special kind of word in the Japanese language that tells readers to pause. In English, the pause can be marked with punctuation, such as a dash. It can also be left unmarked, as in the poem on page 13. In that poem, the end of the second line is a natural place to pause because it marks the end of the first complete thought.

ost haiku use simple words. They are often written in **sentence fragments** rather than in complete sentences. Most haiku are written in the **present tense**. As you read the next poem, notice that it seems to be taking place right now.

Writing in the present tense helps readers feel as if they are experiencing the moment portrayed in the poem. When we read this poem, we feel as if we are watching a flower as it opens its petals for the first time.

Almost-open bud
faces the springtime sun—
Life!

Like the poem on page 17 about a flower bud opening, most haiku are about nature. They don't tell about nature in general, **abstract** terms, though. Each poem presents a specific image of the natural world. Well-written haiku are almost like photographs of a single moment. They show readers what the poet experienced.

In order to bring their experiences to life, haiku poets present a scene just as they came across it. They use their senses. They might write about how a scene looked, sounded, smelled, tasted, or even felt. But they usually do not tell how they felt about what they saw—or how readers should feel about it. They let readers decide that on their own. Notice the use of the senses in the following poem. How does this haiku make you feel?

Snow-silenced trees
shake heavy limbs—
a wet plop

In addition to providing specific images of nature, most Japanese haiku contain a season word, or *kigo*, to let readers know exactly when the poem takes place. In Japanese, season words can be as simple as the name of a season. Or season words can be taken from a special list of words that describe the seasons. This list includes words such as "seeds" for spring, "billowing clouds" for summer, "fog" for fall, and "icy moon" for winter.

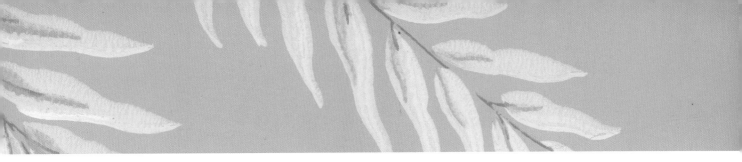

Although poets of haiku in English often use season words as well, there is no specific list of English-language season words. This is partly because the seasons are different in different parts of the English-speaking world. For example, people who live in Alaska probably picture winter quite differently from those who live in Florida!

In their presentation of nature and seasonal imagery, haiku often link two separate images in some way. Sometimes, putting two images together helps readers see their similarities. At other times, it helps to show their differences, as in the poem to the right by Basho.

Here, Basho contrasts the life of summer grass with the death of the ancient warriors who once fought upon it. If Basho had changed the first line to "dying grass," this contrast would have been lost.

The summer grass!
'Tis all that's left
Of ancient warriors' dreams

Haiku are often written in a serious **tone**. But poems with a lighthearted or slightly humorous tone are also common. Haiku are not meant to teach lessons or answer deep questions about life. Instead, the goal of a haiku is to help readers experience a single, brief moment in a new way.

Elizabeth Mowry PSA

Haiku is not the only type of modern poetry to come out of the ancient Japanese art of renga. Another kind of short poem, called *senryu*, got its start from the middle parts of a renga. The structure of a senryu is nearly identical to the structure of a haiku, although senryu often don't have a cutting word.

Senryu also do not usually contain a season word and are not about nature. Instead, they are about human nature, or the way people think and act. While some senryu are serious, many are humorous. They might make fun of people's habits or the way people relate to one another. For example, what do you think the poem to the right is saying about human nature?

He laughs, too—
not understanding
he's the joke

In Japan, haiku and senryu developed out of renga. In the West, the process worked in the reverse order. As some Western haiku poets looked for ways to expand the form, they began to write renga. Today, some renga poets gather together to write their poems. Others write renga through the mail. Each poet writes a verse and then sends the renga to the next poet, who builds on the ideas of the previous writer.

Other haiku poets wanting to expand the form on their own have written longer poems consisting of several stanzas of haiku. Some of the poems present several different views of the same subject. The verses can be read in any order and still make sense. Other poems consist of verses that are meant to be read together in a particular order. Each stanza adds to the meaning of the poem. As you read the poem on the next page, think about the impression you get from the whole poem. Now read each stanza as a separate haiku. Do the images you see change?

The sun burns fast

John Doe
11 County Road
New City, New York

Picking tomatoes
from the first-year garden—
slugs

His finger traces
Blemishes and tracks
across the reddened skin

Hot sun
against a cool breeze—
hint of rain

As you read haiku and its many variations, you may learn to look at the world through fresh eyes. You might find yourself smiling at the sight of a slow-moving cloud. Or maybe you'll feel an ache over the deep loneliness of being surrounded by thick fog. If so, the haiku poet has done his or her job. The poet has made you feel an emotion by presenting you with a brief image. And you can take that feeling into the other types of poetry you read, letting their images and ideas speak to you in new ways.

1. *Playing with syllables.* In order to get used to the length of haiku, it can sometimes help to start by counting syllables. Think of a specific image. Now write about that image in three lines of five, seven, and five syllables. After you're done, **revise** your haiku. Don't worry about syllables this time. Decide which words you want to change or cut. When you're done, read both versions of your haiku. Which do you like better?

2. *Sensing haiku.* When writing haiku, it is important to observe the world with your senses. Spend some time sitting outside. Make a list of what you see, hear, smell, taste, and feel. Now, turn what you have sensed into several haiku. You could write one haiku about each sense. Or, you could combine the senses in unique ways. When you are done, show your haiku to your family or friends and ask how the poems make them feel.

Donegan, Patricia. *Haiku Activities: Asian Arts & Crafts for Creative Kids*. Boston: Tuttle Publishing, 2003.

Gollub, Matthew. *Cool Melons—Turn to Frogs! The Life and Poems of Issa*. New York: Lee & Low Books, 1998.

Lewis, J. Patrick. *Black Swan/White Crow*. New York: Atheneum Books for Young Readers, 1995.

Spivak, Dawnine. *Grass Sandals: The Travels of Basho*. New York: Atheneum Books for Young Readers, 1997.

GLOSSARY

abstract—unable to be defined or described by the senses

imagery—descriptive words that cause people to imagine what something looks like

middle class—people who are not the poorest or the richest; they have an average amount of money

present tense—expressing that an action or event is taking place right now

revise—to rewrite and change

sentence fragments—incomplete sentences; they might be missing a subject (person) or a verb (action)

stanzas—groups of lines that make up a separate part of a poem; verses

syllables—complete units of sound that make up words; for example "sit" has one syllable, and "si-lent" has two

tone—the general attitude or feeling of a poem or story; tone can be serious, playful, or sarcastic

West—the part of the world that includes the U.S. and Europe

BIBLIOGRAPHY

Bowers, Faubion, ed. *The Classic Tradition of Haiku: An Anthology*. Mineola, N.Y.: Dover Publications, 1996.

Brewer, Robert Lee. "Haiku: The Soul of Brevity." *Writer's Digest* 88, no. 1 (February 2008): 83–84.

Higginson, William, with Penny Harter. *The Haiku Handbook: How to Write, Share, and Teach Haiku*. New York: McGraw-Hill Book Company, 1985.

McGraw, H. Ward, ed. *Prose and Poetry for Enjoyment*. Chicago: L. W. Singer Co., 1935.

Sato, Hiroaki. *One Hundred Frogs: From Renga to Haiku to English*. New York: Weatherhill, 1983.

van den Heuvel, Cor, ed. *The Haiku Anthology: Haiku and Senryu in English*. New York: W. W. Norton & Company, 1999.

INDEX